When the Drumbeat Changes, Dance a Different Dance

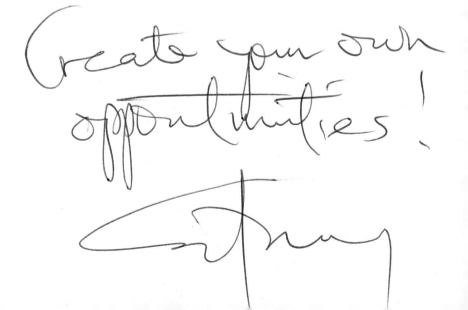

Pat,

Create your own opportunities!

When the Drumbeat Changes, Dance a Different Dance

How to Be
An Opportunist
In Today's
Changing
World

Albert Mensah

AVIVA
PUBLISHING

When the Drumbeat Changes, Dance a Different Dance

Copyright © 2000 by Albert A. Mensah

Albert Mensah
P.O. Box 94308
Seattle, WA 98124-6608

www.questforyourbest.com

ISBN 1-890427-99-3

Editor/Production Coordinator: Tim Polk

Cover Design: Dunn+Associates

Typesetting: Ad Graphics, Inc.

Printed in the United States of America

First Edition

4 6 8 10

This book is dedicated to
my wife Tanya, my soul-mate, partner, and lover.
I adore you. I love you.

My son Joshua (the buu-buu man).
You are the Ashanti son I always wanted.
I am proud of you.

My daughter Ana (my sweet little princess).
You will always be my sweet little princess.

To my parents,
for always believing in my dreams.

To my brothers and sisters,
for their love and support.

Thanks

The author would like to thank the following people for their help in the creation of this book.

Jack Barnard – I love you mannnnn!

Vickie Sullivan – You are the best!

Eileen Geithman – Please don't ever leave!

Laurie Larsen – Thank you for opening my eyes to my passion.

Tim Polk – Thank you for making this book possible. Are you ready for book number two?

Jim Weems – Thank you for the typesetting.

Susan Kendrick – Thank you for your writing.

Dunn + Associates – Thank you for the wonderful cover design.

Dottie Walters – Thank you for all your support.

Rosita Perez – God bless you always.

Nancy Coey – God bless you always.

John Alston – Thank you so much for sharing.

Vanna Novak – Thank you for your help.

Rob Sommer – You are the best!

Chris and Carol Bodlovic – Thank you for being there for me.

Carolyn Kalil – I am following my True Colors and doing the work I love—thank you!

Special Thanks

The author would also like to thank the following for their support.

Toastmasters, Bank Of America Auto Group, Weyerhaeuser, Alaska Airlines, The United States Army, The United States Navy, Costco, Shopnow.com, Head Start Child Development Council, Multnomah County Department of Community Justice, and the many other clients I have spoken to or otherwise assisted over the years.

And thank you, readers,
for the Opportunity to share my message with you.

Table of Contents

Foreword

Albert Mensah and Albert Einstein agree. Einstein said: **"I look and see what others see. Then I think thoughts others have never thought."**

The little boy, Albert Mensah, who had such a longing for the opportunity to use the gifts God gave him, heard the drums of possibility pounding, calling to him: "Wake up! Wake up! Step forward."

Often our ability to hear the drums others do not hear is dulled until we can barely make out the pattern of the beat. What causes the deadening deafness?

It is listening to nay-sayers. "Who do you think you are?" "You don't have the talent to do that." "You haven't got a chance...so why try?"

If we listen to negative people, we may start to think that they know what they are talking about. Listening to them makes them louder. Finally, the drums of opportunity fade away.

However, believe me, I know the drums of opportunity are still pounding as strong as they have for all the generations that have created better lives since the beginning of time. Albert Einstein, Winston Churchill, Helen Keller, and millions of other great minds were thrown out of schools as too stupid to teach. They were told they were too dumb to learn!

Remember, no one knows what you are capable of but you.

My Scottish grandfather taught me this: Grandpa said the drums would always be with me. All I had to do was to put my fingers on the veins of my wrist to feel them, to hear them calling out to me, "Get up!"

He sang this song to me about the drums of opportunity to me when I was a wee girl:

> *"I hear the bagpipes coming!*
>
> *I hear the drummers drumming!*
>
> *My heart replies—thrum thruming.*
>
> *Scotland the Brave!"*

In every race of people on this earth, some hear the drums of opportunity. Some turn off the nay-sayers and succeed. Some are knocked down, bleed a bit, but get up and fight again. Those who hear are doers, the creators, the leaders.

Some are brave, and come marching forward to the beat of the drums.

Is it you?

If so, read on.

— Dottie Walters, CSP
International speaker, author, and consultant

Introduction

Se wo pe se wo daye bamua sore.
"If you want to live your dream,
then you have to wake up."

— African Proverb

On August 21, 1999, I stood on the platform with eight other professional speakers awaiting the Toastmasters World Championship of Public Speaking results. One by one others' names were called until only two people were left—another person and myself. I was excited beyond belief! This is what I had been dreaming about and working toward ever since I had started professional speaking: to be the best!

And then...my name was called. Second place! But I wasn't elated or happy or even satisfied. I was upset! Why? I WANTED TO WIN! In all my self-motivating thoughts and dreams before and during the competition, I always saw myself *winning*. Nobody remembers a second place finisher, right?

Well, I accepted my second place trophy wearing a frown. And I wore that frown as I walked to the table where my wife and others were sitting. When my wife tried to comfort me, I shot her a nasty look! I'm certain that you've heard the saying "If looks could kill." Well, I'm not saying my look right then could have killed someone, but I certainly believed I could've injured a few people!

And do you know what? I was still angry ten minutes later when the program ended. People came to my table to congratulate me, but I brushed them off. I didn't want their well wishes. I wanted to wallow in my own self-pity at not having won.

But then something happened. A woman came up to me with a broad smile on her face. I stood up to greet her, hoping that I'd only have to shake her hand and offer an obligatory "thanks" so that she'd go away. Instead she hugged me and said, "Your speech really hit home with me. I feel like a new person. Thank you!"

As that woman walked away, I realized something: I had forgotten why I had come to the Toastmasters competition—even why I had become a professional speaker—in the first place. It wasn't to win awards. It wasn't to "beat" all the other professional speakers in the world. No, it was to share my message with whoever it was that was listening to me. It was to connect with people; to convey my ideas and insights in a way that would help others reach their goals, to help others become the person that they wanted to become.

When that woman walked away from me, I woke up. It was an amazing feeling.

And that's what I want to accomplish with this book: To help you wake up to your greatest potential and dreams. To send your morale and inspiration soaring. To help you appreciate everything that you have: at home, at work, and in your daily life. To do this, I will share my stories, my beliefs, and my suggestions about leading a life worth living. I will help you not only create good, meaningful goals, but to work toward them in a positive, abundance-mentality fashion. I will help you dream....

Everything starts with a dream. I've had many dreams in my life. You'll hear about some of them in the pages of this book. One of the greatest dreams I ever had was to come to America. You see, I grew up in Ghana, West Africa. It's a beautiful country, but also a very poor one. Opportunities there are few; dreams are hard to believe in. But I made my dream come true, and now I have lived in the United States for more than twenty years.

And do you know what? I'm still dreaming.... Many of my dreams, like coming to and living in America, have come true. Others I'm still working toward. But throughout my life, everyone's life, there's been one constant: change. The world is changing every single day. You, and everyone around you, are changing (or should be). Change won't stop. In fact, it's a good bet it won't even slow down, but instead continue to speed-up, to accelerate faster and faster and faster.

The person who wants to dream and succeed must constantly address and overcome change. This is essential to achieving success "on the inside and the outside", as I like to say.

Are you ready to wake up?

Are you ready to face change?

Are you ready to dream...and succeed?

I hope so!

Let's go!

Albert Mensah
Seattle, WA
April 2000

CHAPTER 1

Opportunity is a Choice

In 1978, shortly after I arrived in the United States, I was standing in line at a bank in New York City. I'm nervous. Why? I'm eighteen years old and it's the first time I've been inside a bank. And this just isn't any bank. It's one of those huge, grand ones in New York City. Plus I'm wearing an *adinkra,* a brightly colored robe from my country. My *adinkra* is formal wear in Ghana, but not in New York City. Of the thirty or so people ahead of me in line, I'm the only one wearing an *adinkra.*

And there's more. We immigrants like to band together. There are thirty-two of us there at the bank. Thirty-one are standing off to the side. I've been elected spokesperson, so I'm in line.

Finally it's my turn. I approach the teller and ask in a loud voice heavy with an accent, "Hello, how do I open up a bank account?"

The teller looks at me like I'm from another world. Granted, I have an accent, and I'm wearing my *adinkra,* and thirty-one of my friends, also in *adinkras,* are looking anxiously our way. But I'm still a person, right?

Not according to the teller. I quickly see that she sees me as a problem. I can almost hear her thoughts: *I need to get rid of this guy, and quick.* So this teller does what most people would do: She calls her manager and passes me off to him.

The bank manager takes me to his desk. I sit down, and again I say, "Hello, how do I open up a bank account."

Immediately I see that the bank manager views me as a problem, too. He acts uncomfortable. He doesn't want to get involved, to help. He says, "I'll be right back," and leaves.

So I sit there and wait. And wait.... And wait some more....

And do you know what? That bank manager never returned. I felt very uncomfortable sitting there. People were staring at my beautiful *adinkra*, staring at me. A black man wearing a brightly colored *adinkra* in a New York City bank. *He must be a problem*, the other people in line seemed to be saying.

Do you know what I did? I walked out. My friends came with me, too. But we didn't moan or complain, and we certainly didn't quit trying to open up a bank account. We went to another bank. Again I stood in line. And again when it was my turn, I asked the teller how to open up a new account. This teller smiled when I made my request. "Step over to that desk and I'll help you," she said.

And that's what she did. She patiently answered my questions, gave me the appropriate forms to fill out, explained what type of identification I needed to open an account. She treated me like a fellow human being.

What happened with this teller versus the first teller?

Had my accent gone away? No.

Had I changed my clothes? No—I was still wearing my *adinkra*.

Had my friends left me? No—all thirty-one were still standing off to the side.

Was I different? No.

But the teller was. When I asked to open up a bank account, the second teller didn't see a problem, she saw an opportunity.

The next day, my friends returned to that same bank and each one of them opened a new account. In two days, that bank got thirty-two new, separate accounts. And do you know what? Twenty years later, many of us still have those accounts. And not only that, during those twenty years that bank made a lot of money from us. A lot! We opened up checking and savings accounts; we took out home mortgages; we applied for and were approved for business loans; we brought our friends and family members there. *You need a bank? I know just the place!*

I can almost hear you asking, *So what, Albert?*

Well, my point is this: The teller at the first bank saw me as a problem. And because she saw me as a problem, she treated me as a problem. Her manager also saw me as a problem, and he treated me as one, too.

But the second teller saw me as an opportunity. Yes, I spoke with an accent and dressed differently than most New Yorkers and I wasn't certain how things worked. But that second teller looked beyond the differences, and instead focused on the opportunities. And her efforts, and the bank's, have been rewarded thousands of times over during the past twenty years.

What one person saw as a problem, another saw as an opportunity.

The choice is always ours.

Reflective Exercise

Can you think of a time when you automatically viewed a person or event as a problem, when this same person or event could have been an opportunity? Describe the situation:

_____

_____

_____

In the future, what can you do to prevent your "automatic" reaction?

_____

_____

_____

Coming to America

Opportunity has always been a major theme of my life. I think one of the main reasons for this is because I grew up in a place where there was so little opportunity. Life was (and still is for most) a struggle. But even though times were bad, and opportunities weren't abundant, I still believed in opportunity, and I still followed it when it did present itself.

Here's another story about opportunity.

I first knew I wanted to come to America at age eight. My family had just moved from a remote village to Accra, the capital. Walking around the city, my head was filled with sights and sounds I had never seen or heard before. One was an advertisement for a movie. I had never seen a movie. I had never seen a movie theater, or watched a television show. I wanted to go!

At my urging (pleading was more like it!), my father took me to see my first movie. It was an American film. I was dazzled by everything I saw: the tall buildings, the shiny new cars, the fact that everyone wore shoes!

I knew right then that I wanted to go to America.

But it wasn't because of the things that I saw. No, even at my young age, I saw and was dazzled by something else: opportunity. In America, it seemed to be everywhere. And even better, in America it seemed to be available to everyone.

Now that I've lived in the United States for more than twenty years, I'm more certain than ever that America *is* the Land of Opportunity. It's not perfect, of course. It has its flaws, people and things we'd all like to change if possible. Still, America is the best country in the world, the most prosperous and advanced nation in history.

But if this is true, if opportunities here are so abundant, why do so many people complain? Why do they criticize? Why do they ignore the opportunities?

Because these people don't want to do the hard work necessary to succeed. They are given opportunities, but they also want to be given the fruits of success *without first working toward and for success.*

That's not how the world works. Not here, in America. Not in West Africa. Not anywhere.

How to Be an Opportunist

I think the word "opportunity" is the most powerful word in the English language. In Webster's Dictionary, opportunity is defined as *a favorable juncture of circumstances, a good chance for advancement or progress.*

That's a good definition, but it doesn't have enough juice for me, enough pizzazz. Here's my definition:

> *Opportunity:*
> **The gift God gave us to have a full-tilt boogie life.**

How's that for pizzazz? Does the word opportunity get you excited now? It should!

There's another word closely related to "opportunity" that I strongly believe in, and that word is "opportunist." The dictionary says that an opportunist *is one who takes advantage of opportunities* **with little regard for principles or consequences**.

Notice the words in bold type. That's not a positive thing to say about someone, is it? No. In fact, an opportunist by Mr. Webster's definition has a negative connotation. *Albert's an opportunist, that scoundrel.*

But I don't agree with Mr. Webster. I think he's giving opportunism a bad name. Here's my definition:

Opportunist: One who knows that there are rampant opportunities everywhere to make your dreams come true.

As you can see, I use the word opportunist in the most positive sense possible. I call myself an opportunist. It's even printed on my business card!

What's more, I think you should call yourself one, too. Be an opportunist! It's critical to making your dreams come true.

There are three key elements to being an effective opportunist:

1. Believing in opportunity
2. Seeing opportunity
3. Acting on opportunity

Believing in Opportunity

Before you can use or acquire something, you must first believe that it exists. It's my belief, one that I hope you share, that all of us in America live in the Land of Opportunity. As I said before, America isn't perfect, but there are opportunities everywhere. Opportunities are why people risk life and limb to get here, whether it's hidden in a truck illegally crossing the U.S.-Mexico border, or in a boat coming from Cuba... or Haiti... or China....

Believe that opportunities are present, and that they are present for you, and you'll be on the first step to making your dreams come true.

Seeing Opportunity

OK, you say, *I believe there are opportunities in this country. But where are they specifically? How do I find them?*

To see opportunity, you have to open yourself up to the opportunities that are all around us. Here's an example. Take a look at the drawing below. How many squares are there?

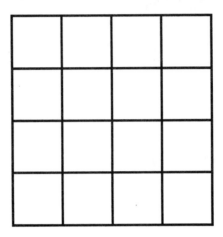

Now count the squares again. Are you still sure about your answer, about what you're seeing?

There are 30 squares. They're all there. There are:

- 1 large square
- 16 small squares of 1 square each
- 4 squares of 9 squares each
- 9 squares of 4 squares each

Most people will only see the 16 small squares; they will not have counted—"seen"—the other squares. If you saw all 30, great!—you're probably already good at seeing opportunity. But if you didn't see the extra squares, maybe it's time to work on your "seeing" skills. You see, just as we overlook many of the squares in the diagram, we also overlook opportunities that are "right there" in front of us.

Still not convinced? Then try what I call my "classified theory." Find a newspaper of the largest city that you live near. Buy a copy of this newspaper. Open it up to the classified section. Do you know what's listed there? That's right: jobs. And jobs and more jobs. Each one of those jobs, no matter if it's for a minimum wage position or a six-figure executive salary, is an opportunity. I guarantee you'll see more opportunities in that newspaper than are available to entire populations of people in distant lands.

You must train your mind, your eyes, and your brain to "see" opportunity everywhere.

Acting on Opportunity

I believe that opportunity is always knocking at the door. *Knock, knock, knock!* That's opportunity knocking.

That's great, of course, but you have to answer the door to let in the opportunities. Believing in opportunity is vital, as is seeing opportunity. But a final, absolutely essential element is to *act* on an opportunity when it presents itself.

That's a key: Action! An Opportunist doesn't sit back and hope that something happens. He takes action.

Let's talk about the classified section of the newspaper again. There are jobs everywhere. But not one of those companies advertising available jobs is going to call you up and invite you in for interview out of the blue. You have to take the first step, to take action. First you will have to mail or fax your resume, or go fill-out an application in person, or call a phone number for more information.... Something. But regardless of what must be done first, only you can do it.

Only when you take action and move toward an opportunity will the opportunity begin to have a chance of coming true.

Reflective Exercise

Think of a time when you didn't treat someone in the "right" way. What happened?

_____

_____

_____

What was the missed opportunity?

_____

_____

_____

Now sit and think for a few minutes about opportunities that are all around you, but that you may not have been "seeing" before. Write these down.

_____

_____

From the list you just made, circle one opportunity and describe what action you are going to take to make the opportunity a reality.

_____

_____

_____

A Final Note

As I've said, I believe opportunity is a choice. We must believe it, see it, and act on it.

And here's something else to consider, to understand: There are two dimensions this action can take. One is what you want for yourself; who you want to become, the dreams that you want to reach. The second dimension is what you want for your world. Everyday you have the opportunity to create the life of your dreams and you have the ongoing chance to better the world. I call this the Opportunity of a Lifetime.

Every one of us has the power to change the world. Hundreds of times a day you have the opportunity to treat family, friends, and strangers the way you would like to be treated. You have the opportunity to create the kind of world that you want to live in, be a proud part of. More important than money or success or winning first place at Toastmasters is the quality of your life.

Again, it all comes down to choices.

Your biggest opportunities in life are about kindness and compassion. Every fear faced, every prejudice removed, every obstacle overcome makes you—and the world—better.

And if you ignore these choices? If you stumble or grumble your way through the world seeking "success," what happens? You've experienced what I call a Missed Opportunity. This Missed Opportunity isn't about achieving fame or building a fortune; it's about bettering the world in ways small and large.

I know what you're probably saying right now: *But Albert, I can't change things that much. And besides, what does this have to do with my dreams, my goals?*

My answer: EVERYTHING! If you train yourself to believe in opportunity, to see it when it knocks, and to take action when it presents itself, you will achieve the life that you've dreamed about <u>and</u> you will make a major difference in the world.

Your dreams may lead to fame, fortune, success. I hope they do. In fact, I urge you to GO FOR IT! But at the same time, every one of us has an ongoing opportunity to add compassion and understanding to the world, and to do so every single day. If you fail to do this, you are missing the opportunity of a lifetime, regardless of the personal fame and riches that come your way.

NOTES

CHAPTER 2

The Power of Dreams and Goals

In the previous chapter, I frequently referred to a person's dreams and goals. In this chapter, I'd like to expand on dreams and goals and explain how I believe they are essential for the person interested in living a fulfilling, successful life.

The Powers of Dreams

A *dream* is what a person wants to be, become, or achieve in the future. It's the big-picture, a vision, and usually can be summed up in a few words or a short sentence.

I want to write novels.

I want to play professional baseball.

I want to marry and have two children.

I want to leave Ghana and come to America.

That last one was mine. Remember in the previous chapter when I watched that American movie, and saw all the opportunity? I knew right then that one day I wanted to go to America, live here, and be a part of it and all the opportunities available. That was my dream.

Everything begins with a dream.

But what makes up a dream? What's important? Here are elements I believe all worthwhile dreams must have:

- **It must be *your* dream.** Notice in the previous examples that the sentences didn't say, *My father wants me to play professional baseball*, or, *My husband wants me to marry (him) and have two children.* You can share your dream with others, and they can help you achieve your dreams, but the dream must be yours.

- **The dream must be important to you.** Weak dreams are like a weak fire; they both throw off weak heat. I've had many people say to me, *But Albert, I don't know if this is what I* really *want to do? How can I be sure?* You will know if your dream is important to you. You will feel it in your heart and in your gut. It will keep you up at night thinking about it. You may have to put it aside for a few weeks, or even a few years, but it will still be there, inside of you. Important dreams don't die.

- **You must keep the dream alive no matter what.** Dreams are, more often than not, for the long-term. In my case, it took me almost ten years to make my dream of coming to America come true. Did I have some doubts along the way? Yes. Were there obstacles in my path? Of course. But as I fought the doubts and obstacles, I never lost sight of my dream.

What is your dream? Do you have one? You should. If you don't have a dream, how can you make it come true?

**Opportunities are everywhere.
But they are invisible to those who are not
clear about what they want.**

Reflective Exercise

In a quiet place, sit for a few moments and ponder your dreams. Then answer these questions:

What are your one or two most important dreams?

_____

_____

How committed are you to making these dreams come true?

_____

_____

What obstacles are preventing you from achieving these goals?

_____

_____

Are these obstacles ones that can be overcome?

_____

_____

The Power of Goals

When I first knew I wanted to come to America, I also knew that it would be difficult. My family didn't have much money. I didn't have any friends or relatives in America. An entire ocean stood between my home in Ghana and the magical United States.

But I didn't let these obstacles stop me. My dream was to go to America, and I took every action possible to make my dream come true.

One of the things I did was to read as much as I could about America. Often my older brother would take me to the library and help me find books about America. Other times I didn't have a ride, so I walked to the library—four-and-a-half miles, one way. I practically lived at the library.

Later, when my reading and writing improved, I found pen pals in magazines and we wrote back and forth. I learned a lot about the United States from these correspondences. My friends made fun of me because of my obsession with America. They even gave me a nickname: "States."

Later still, I was accepted into the very prestigious St. John's School, a Catholic High School in Ghana run by the Brothers of the Holy Cross, a group of Jesuit priests from the United States. At St. John's, I was able to actually meet Americans and talk with them about the country and share my dream of going there.

So I had done a lot. I had learned a lot. But the obstacles were still there. I didn't have enough money to go to the United States, and I didn't know anyone I could ask to borrow the money.

But I had a dream, and from that dream I developed a goal: I would write to as many colleges and universities in America as it would take for one to offer me a scholarship. That's all I needed: one organization to help me. Could I do it? I believed so.

By the end of my junior year in high school, I had written to 235 American colleges and universities. Most didn't bother to reply. The ones that did offered me a polite "no." All except one. Western Maryland College offered me a full four-year scholarship. I had done it! I was on my way to achieving my dream!

As you can see, my dream of traveling to America was always with me. But I took different steps and pursued various opportunities that would support my dream. These are *goals*.

Here's a more formal definition:

Goals are the desired outcomes that you want to realize or have happen within a set period of time.

Goals are vital to success. They are the steps you must take to reach your dreams. Without good goals, your dream will always remain just that: a dream.

Here are some important things to remember about goals:

- Set SPECIFIC goals. For me, a vague goal would have been something like, "I will seek a way to attend college for free." A much more specific would be, "By the end of my junior year in high school, I will write to every accredited four-year college or university seeking a full scholarship." See how much more specific, hence compelling, the second goal is?

- Set BIG Goals. You have to dream big and think big if you want to be big. Don't set little goals. Stretch yourself. You're as small as your controlling desires, or as great as your dominant aspirations. Always remember this: High expectations ALWAYS precede high achievement.

- Set REALISTIC and ATTAINABLE goals. Don't have a goal of playing professional basketball if you're five feet tall, weigh 110 pounds, and have no athletic ability. If you're overweight, don't set a goal of losing thirty pounds in one week. Rather, set a goal of losing one to two pounds every week for thirty weeks. Be realistic.

- Set TANGIBLE goals. By this I mean, Can you visualize your goal? Can you see it happening? Feel it? Smell it? Hear it? Can you define it? Make your goals tangible, concrete.

- MEASURE your goals. Write down your goals. Are your goals measurable? Is it clear exactly what must happen for a goal to be met? Can you measure progress toward your goals on a daily, weekly, or monthly basis? (Or better yet, all three?)

- Attack your goals with PASSION. A goal is useless if you fail to move toward it. Take action, even if it's a small step toward achieving the goal. And get excited. Have enthusiasm not only about your goal but also about the process of achieving it. Your enthusiasm and determination should be so great that people will notice it when you enter a room. If you can't get *passionate* about your goals, it's time to review your goals.

There's an important word in that last bullet: determination. Chapter Six is all about becoming and staying motivated, but I want to say this now about determination: You must have it to achieve your goals and dreams. Why? Because if you're setting big, far-reaching goals, there will always be obstacles in your way. You will need to overcome these fears, problems, and challenges. The process of achieving your goals and dreams may take weeks or months, and more probably years!

Only when you are determined to achieve your goals and dreams can you persevere when "times get tough." Determination also helps you stay focused on your goals, not get side-tracked by another project or obstacle. Without focus, it's too easy for anyone to get sidetracked in today's complex, constantly changing world.

Reflective Exercise

Are your goals written down? If not, write them on a piece of paper.

Now review your goals. Do they share the traits good goals share?

Are your goals SPECIFIC, BIG, REALISTIC and ATTAINABLE, and TANGIBLE, MEASURABLE?

Are you PASSIONATE about achieving your goals?

Combining Dreams and Goals

As you can see, dreams and goals are closely linked. Once you have a dream, you must create various goals that will move you toward achieving that dream. Everything must work together, everything must fit.

The following exercise will help you see how dreams and goals work together, and how you can begin **today** to move toward your dreams.

Reflective Exercise

What is one dream that you want to make come true? (Let yourself go on this part. Ask yourself, *If money were no object, what would I do with my life?*

_____

_____

Select one element of your vision.

_____

_____

Now list three to five steps or actions you would need to take to make this happen.

_____

_____

State the one action you can take *today* to begin working toward your goals and dream.

_____

Assign time frames to complete the other steps.

_____

And finally, answer this question: To get "on-track" to achieving my goals and dreams, what will I have to give up?

_____

_____

A Final Note

Here's a final thought: When you are setting your dreams and goals, NEVER FIT IN! What do I mean by that? Don't be average, one of the crowd. **Always be outstanding.** By setting big goals and working to achieve them, you will separate yourself from the many, many others who aren't pushing themselves, who have accepted the "status quo."

When I had my dream to come to America, I didn't fit in with most people in my country, particularly the friends I had that were my age. These friends laughed at me. "HA HA HA! That Albert's crazy if he thinks he'll make it to America."

They gave me all the reasons I wouldn't or couldn't make it. Too expensive. Too hard to get a Visa to leave the country. Too far to fly. And so on....

They made fun of me. "That crazy Albert, let's call him 'States.' Yeah, that's his new nickname. 'States.'"

And do you know what? When I had gotten the college scholarship, and obtained my Visa, and saved money for the plane ride to America, do you know what my friends said then? "We knew you could do it, Albert. Oh, and by the way, when you come back, could you bring us some T-shirts? We'd really like some shirts from America."

If your dream is big enough, if you believe in it enough and are passionate enough about making it a reality, your determination will help you persevere.

Don't fit in. Dream big dreams, and create good goals to make those dreams come true.

NOTES

CHAPTER 3

Face Your Snakes

One of my boyhood chores was to walk to the river, collect water in a bucket that I brought with me, and bring the water back for my family before I had to leave for school. No problem, right? But the river was two miles away. That's four miles round-trip. And that's not all: I had to make *two* trips to gather all the water my family needed. I started out every morning at 6:30 a.m. to make it back in time to leave for school. I was late for school a lot in those days!

One morning I'm walking to the river. My sister is with me this time. As we reach the river, she screams, "Watch out Albert! There's a snake!"

I looked down and sure enough, there's a snake. And this isn't some sissy-sized snake. It's a Ghana snake: big, thick, scary. And this snake is twirling and coiling, twisting and turning, and all the time staring right at me. And I'm staring at the snake. The snake is staring at me staring back at him.

I yelled out for my sister to run away. No problem. My sister's no dummy—she's long gone!

So it's just this snake and me, staring at each other.

I knew right then I had a choice to make. I could turn and run and hope that the snake wouldn't catch me. Or I could stay and face the snake like some knight of the Roundtable squaring off against a fire-breathing dragon.

Before I tell you what happened, let me add a couple of things. One, I've been afraid of snakes all my life. Second, I was afraid of *this* snake. And probably most important, before I had always run away from snakes, real and imagined. Every impulse inside of me right then was screaming, *Run, Albert, run!*

But something changed inside me that day. I decided right then that, no matter what, I wasn't going to be afraid of this snake. I wasn't going to run. I was going to face this snake.

So I stared at the snake. He stared back at me. We stared at each other for a long time, or at least it seemed so to me. And do you know what happened? That sissy snake chickened out; he turned and slithered into the water.

I filled my pail and stood tall. I had scared away a snake!

Overcoming Fear

More than thirty years have passed since I stared down that snake. Now if I want water, I turn on the faucet in my kitchen in the home my family and I have in Seattle. Still, that moment with the snake is so fresh in my mind, it's as if it happened yesterday. And I still face snakes all the time. They aren't the slithery kind, of course, they're everyday things like paying bills, satisfying a persnickety client, or helping my two kids do their homework. Everyone faces these types of snakes every day. They're all around us. They will never go away completely.

Reflective Exercise

What are some of the snakes you've been afraid to face?

_____

_____

_____

Are there any snakes you are facing right now that have you frightened? Feeling alone?

_____

_____

_____

What do you think would happen if you faced one of these snakes?

_____

_____

_____

Only when a person learns to face and ultimately overcome their snakes can they then be free to move toward their goals, to accomplish the things that they want to in life, to become the person they want to become.

How does a person do this? Remember the acronym SNAKE:

- **S – Stay Motivated**. There will be many snakes blocking your path to success. Big or little, real or perceived, a person must stay motivated and excited about working at making their goals a reality. Don't take rejection personally. Feed your mind with positive thoughts and new information. Feed your body with nourishing food. Feed your soul with spiritual peace. Surround yourself with positive, supportive friends and family members.

- **N – Never Doubt Yourself**. You can have anything on earth that you want, once you mentally accept the fact that you can have it. If you want a particular success, visualize yourself as having obtained this success. If you want to be a particular type of person, see yourself in your mind as already being this type of person. The feeling of success, your personal vision of it, must come first. Self-confidence is vital to the person striving to achieve goals, to be a better person.

- **A – Act Daily**. The path to success is long. Learn to enjoy the journey. Take daily action toward your goals, even if it's only for five minutes. Most successful people do not achieve success in a sudden burst of genius, a moment of rapture. More likely than not, it has taken years of hard work, practice and commitment. Move forward day by day, step by step.

- **K – Know Your Purpose**. Here's an old saying that you may have heard before: If you don't know where you're going, any road will take you there. How true! Only when you have a clear purpose as to what you want to do, achieve, or become can you move forward in a concise, effective way. Know exactly what it is that you want to accomplish. Make it as clear and exciting as possible.

• **E – Expect Success.** The mind is a wonderful, mysterious organ. It's also extremely powerful. When programmed for success by positive thoughts, it will help create new successes. Expect to succeed. Draw from past successes no matter how small or seemingly insignificant. If you're trying something new, see yourself in your mind succeeding, doing, becoming. Visualize future successes at night before falling asleep, in the morning upon waking, before or after a mid-day meal. Only when you feel success is yours to receive will it be given to you.

Struggling with Snakes

When I confronted that snake as a boy, did you notice what I did? I didn't try to kill that snake, or ever attack it or club it or trick it or anything like that. All I did was face that snake, stand up to it, and it slithered away.

Many times in life, all it takes to eliminate fear (snakes) is to face your fear. As Franklin Roosevelt once said, "Do the thing you fear, and the death of fear is certain."

How does one do this? I have a simple recommendation: Do the thing that you fear as early as possible during the day. Get it over and done with. Then you can move on to other tasks and activities. For example, if you are in sales and you fear making cold calls, make these calls the first thing in the morning. Then spend the rest of your day on more enjoyable activities and tasks. If you are a manager and must meet with an employee whose performance is below expectations, schedule the meeting as early as possible.

Don't procrastinate. If you do, the problem (snake) will simmer and smolder within you.

The most successful people in this world realize that there will always be problems (snakes) big and small. These shouldn't be attacked. But a person should stand up and confront their snakes. When fear is conquered, success will almost certainly follow.

Snakes Never Go Away

After I'd gotten my college scholarship and had scraped together enough money to fly to the United States, I still have another big snake to overcome: that airplane! I'd never seen an airplane before, let alone ridden in one. And now I was going to have to fly more than 3,000 miles in one across an ocean. *Who am I kidding?* I found myself thinking.

But I faced that snake. I went to the airport. I entered the plane. The flight attendant tied me to the seat with rope and put duct tape over my mouth and…. No, it wasn't *that* bad. But I needed a lot of attention from a very nice flight attendant during that twelve-hour flight. Whatever the airline was paying her, she earned it on that trip.

The point I want to make is that snakes never totally go away. As you climb each rung on the ladder of success, you will meet new challenges, be presented with new obstacles, face more and different snakes.

Once a person realizes this, facing the snakes become much easier. Think how boring life would be if there was no challenge, no opportunity. Challenges (snakes) must be met to achieve our goals and dreams? Why *not* overcome these as quickly and as painlessly as possible?

Reflective Exercise

Write down your "snakes": your biggest, scariest fears. Don't hold anything back.

_____

_____

_____

Now answer this question: What new opportunities would open up to you if you faced your fears?

_____

_____

_____

Pick one snake, a big one. What are two ways you can face this snake *today*?

_____

_____

_____

Snakes can be faced with a little faith and a lot of practice. Here are four examples of people who faced huge snakes…and still prevailed.

- Alexandra Solzhenitzyn wrote *Gulag Archipelago* in a Siberian prison on pieces of paper no bigger than a large postage stamp.

- Nelson Mandela sat in a prison cell for twenty-seven years because of his beliefs. Think of it! But instead of souring, he kept his principles and remained true to his purpose, bringing apartheid to a halt. When he was released from prison, he became the leader of his country.

- It took Raymond Carver, one of this country's most respected short-story writers, 16 years to have his first collection of stories published. When his children were young, he used to sit in his car to find a quiet place to write.

- Christopher Reeve had everything: dashing looks, a Hollywood movie career, a wonderful family. One day while riding a horse he fell and was paralyzed from the neck down. If anyone had a reason to be depressed, to curse God, he did. But Christopher Reeve saw an opportunity, and pursued it, and now is a spokesperson with a charge to increase public awareness about spinal cord injuries and to help raise money for research into a cure.

Do you see the "snakes" in each person's life just mentioned? How do your snakes compare? They faced their snakes; are you willing to face yours?

A Final Note: The 4 a.m. Wake-up Call

As I've said, snakes will never go completely away. Just like change is a constant in our world, so too are problems, obstacles, difficulties.

I still face snakes. Every day. People say, "Albert, you're heading for the top," or, "Albert, already Toastmasters says you're the second-best speaker in the world—you've got it made."

But those thoughts don't help me when I wake up at four o'clock in the morning, thinking, worried. Will I have enough clients? Will I have *too many* clients? Will people like this book? Will the critics and professional reviewers give it high marks? Why did I quit my six-figure sales career to become a professional speaker? Am I saving enough for my two kids' college education? (Let me tell you, that's a *big* snake my wife and I will face in the future.)

Being an Opportunist in this changing world is a challenge for everyone, even those who are succeeding. I call these snakes and challenges the "4 a.m. wake-up call." I still do my share of gnashing and gnarling, of waking up at four o'clock in the morning and thinking, *What have I done? Have I bitten off too much?*

But I do know one thing: I won't let any obstacle, no matter how big, stop me. It may slow me down a bit until I figure out how to overcome it. But I will face that obstacle and, in the long run, I will conquer it.

There are opportunities behind every obstacle.

Face your snakes.

NOTES

CHAPTER 4

Opportunity + DESIRE = Success

We've talked a lot about opportunity to this point. But if opportunity is everywhere, available in one degree or another to all, why isn't *everyone* successful? Why is success still so difficult to achieve, so hard to come by? Above all, what sets apart the successful person from the unsuccessful one, the winner from the whiner?

I believe there are key six traits that every person must understand and possess to take an opportunity and succeed. Together these traits spell DESIRE. Each is critical to personal and professional success.

The DESIRE Formula

When opportunities are combined with what I call the DESIRE Formula, successes of the highest levels are possible. The DESIRE Formula is as follows:

- **D—DESIRE**. A person must know exactly what it is that they want out of life. I tell my audiences and the people I coach, "Opportunities are everywhere, but they are invisible to those who aren't clear about what they want." Be as specific as possible about what it is that you want. Know this is true in your head—and your heart. And remember this, weak desires create weak results. The degree of your desire is the power with which your energies will be directed.

- **E—EDUCATION**. African proverb: Lack of knowledge is darker than the night. I firmly believe this. A person must become an information sponge, learning something new and exciting every single day to help fuel their desire and move toward their goals. How does one do this? Visit libraries and bookstores for motivational books, audio tapes, and videos. Take an evening class at a local college or through a community workshop. Learn about and use the Internet. Find a mentor, someone successful you can meet with and learn from. The opportunities to learn are endless.

- **S—SELF-CONFIDENCE**. Believing in yourself is critical to achieving success. Self-confidence is difficult to acquire, especially when you are attempting something new. There's risk involved, a fear of failure, of looking foolish. At my first few public speaking engagements, I was scared! Here's a secret: Self-confidence builds with practice, commitment. If you work hard to make your goals come true, your self-confidence will grow as you grow. It won't be easy. But you will reach a point where you will know in your heart that you can accomplish what you set out to do.

- **I—INTEGRITY**. When I first saw that American movie and knew that I wanted to come to America, I quickly discovered there were several small obstacles in my way, and one big one: the Atlantic Ocean. I couldn't swim across, so I had to either sail or fly. There were no shortcuts, in other words. The same is true with success. You can't walk over others on the way to the top. Whatever you do should be done with integrity. Do what you say, say what you mean. There are no shortcuts to the top.

- **R—RESPONSIBILITY**. Success requires that you accept responsibility for your thoughts and actions. Nobody else can think positive thoughts for you, take the steps needed to reach your goals. Only you can make success happen. You are the only person who can live your life.

- **E—ENTHUSIASM**. A final element of the DESIRE formula is *enthusiasm*, positive thoughts and actions on your part about what you are doing and where you are going. Why is enthusiasm so important? Because you will face obstacles big and small almost every single day on the journey to success. One of these obstacles will be doubt, doubt in your abilities, in what you are striving to achieve. But enthusiasm will help overcome the obstacles, help you stay positive and focused on creating solutions rather than wallowing in pity, in the problems. Start the day enthusiastic, go through the day this way, and end each day on a positive note.

I'd like to expand on one of the points just mentioned: Integrity. You have to live the life that you want to, that you want others to be proud of. When opportunities present themselves, you must make choices. You must decide based on integrity, on having sound priorities.

It isn't always easy.

One wrong choice I made STILL bothers me.

When my wife was pregnant with our first child, we got up one morning and she said, "Albert, honey, I think my water broke."

Now up to this point in my life, the only pregnant woman I'd ever been around before was my mama, and the only time I'd heard the term "water broke" was when my sister dropped the bucket on the way back from the river. I didn't have any idea what that term meant as far as being pregnant.

I also was distracted that morning. At the time, I was selling Yellow Pages advertising. I had been trying to line up a meeting with a potentially huge client for months, and finally he agreed to meet. The big meeting was that morning.

I had a choice to make. I decided not to ask too many questions to my wife. I told her, "Let me go do my appointment and I'll be back."

So I went to my office to pick up some paperwork and ran into my boss. She asked me about Tanya, my wife, and I said, "She's fine, although she did say this morning that her water broke. I guess we'll have to go to the doctor later and check it out. After my meeting, of course."

I added that last part hoping to impress my boss. She knew I had that big meeting that morning. I was going to bring in a major new account!

But my boss was upset. "What are you doing here at work?" she said. "You go home right now and take care of your wife!"

So I hurried home and found my wife lying in bed, moaning. "Oh…oh…oh…oh…my God!"

I thought she was going to die. I called the ambulance, and when the medics arrived one said, "She's definitely dilated."

Here was another term I had no idea what it meant. My poor wife! Dilated!

They rushed her to the hospital. Luckily things turned out fine. My wife did have a Cesarean, but our son was born healthy, and my wife had no complications.

Later, when the doctor found out what had happened, he called me aside. "Albert, if something had happened to your wife, if you'd lost your baby, what would you have said to your wife? 'Sorry, honey, but this big meeting was more important than you.'"

That doctor was right.

As you know, I made a wrong choice that day when my wife's water broke. In fact, I've made wrong choices more times than I care to admit. But I've also learned from almost every one of these instances. And that's the key: act with integrity, but when you catch yourself stumbling, when the choice you made wasn't the right one, stop and learn from it. Feel the pain your wrong decision caused, both to you and others. Think what you could have or should have done differently.

Your priorities determine your choices. I didn't have my head on straight that day, and the results could've been disastrous.

Reflective Exercise

Think back to a time when you were faced with a critical decision, a choice between conflicting-but-important decisions.

Did you make the right choice, the choice with integrity?

_____

_____

Why or why not?

_____

_____

_____

What did you learn from this situation?

_____

_____

_____

A Final Note

Here is an African proverb that resonates with the material in this chapter:

Monkey says, "If you keep your child in front of you, you can see what is the matter with it."

What does that mean? It means that you are responsible for your own affairs. Remember the R in DESIRE? Responsibility.

Throughout this book, we talk about opportunity and success, about dreams and goals, taking action and following through. Do you notice a common thread these topics all share? No one can do any of these things except you. Yes, others may help you along the way, in some cases significantly. But the responsibility always ultimately rests with you...to dream, to do, to succeed.

NOTES

CHAPTER 5

When the Drumbeat Changes...

"Life is change.
Growth is optional.
Choose wisely."

— Author Unknown

In early January 2000, I went into my local copy shop. There on the counter was a stack of nice new calendars for the year. The copy shop had printed its name and telephone number on the calendar, and was giving them away free to clients. I picked up the top calendar, opened it to January, and saw a beautiful picture of a towering spruce tree completely covered in pure white snow.

I also saw the quote that appears at the top of this page.

Talk about a changing world, right? On January 1, 2000, we experienced a new year, a new decade, and a new millenium.

Change is all around us, right? Stop and think about this for a moment: Ten years ago, how likely was it that you:

- had or saw others using cellular phones?

- accessed e-mail on something called the Internet?

- owned a personal computer capable of holding 200+ megabytes of memory?

- used a fax machine?

- heard of a company called Microsoft...or Starbucks...or Yahoo!...or Amazon.com?

- paid $.33 to mail a first-class piece of mail anywhere in the United States?

Change is happening all around us, every day, almost (it seems) at every moment. While change can be invigorating, even exhilarating, it also can be disconcerting, even frightening. Change forces us to do new things, learn new things, adapt...or be left behind.

Throughout this book we've discussed the choices you can make in your life. To see opportunities...to create dreams and goals...to help others. This is probably the most important choice you will ever face: to accept that change is inevitable, and that only by choosing to flow with change, rather than oppose it, will we grow and prosper.

Handling Change

How can a person embrace, rather than shrink from, change? Consider the following ideas and suggestions:

- Know that there will be rough times. Dealing with change can be difficult. It can cause interruptions in the way we live, work, and play—it disrupts our comfort level, in other words. Don't worry if your mind or body reacts negatively to change. Accept this "push back," then attempt to move forward.

- Focus on the positive. Often when a change happens, we focus on the potential negative aspects of the change rather the potential positives. A transfer to a new department within your organization may be stressful, but it may also bring with it new opportunities for advancement.

- Listen to your body, heart, mind and soul. Often one of the worse aspects of change is the uncertainty. Should I do *this* instead of *that*? Should I quit my job? Should I do...well, you get the picture. As much as possible, listen to what your body, heart, mind, and soul are saying to you; the "answer" is almost certainly inside you.

This last point is an important one. Let me tell you a story of a time when I was resisting change, with negative consequences.

I had been working for the phone company for 12 years, primarily selling Yellow Pages advertising. I had done extremely well: consistently beating quotas, being ranked the number one sales person in my area, etc.

But then something happened. My dream to become a professional speaker and inspire others took hold within me. For weeks and months I debated about whether professional speaking was something for me, if I could make a solid living at it. Would I have enough to say? Who could help coach me on delivery? How much marketing was involved?

Do you know what happened? After a stellar career at the phone company, during this time of uncertainty my productivity dropped way off. My sales were down; the shine was off my star.

Finally one day my manager called me into her office. She had on her "manager's face," so I knew this was a serious meeting. Anyway, she hit me with a bomb. "Albert, your sales are way off, and we've talked in the past about this and you haven't shown any improvement, so we're going to have to demote you."

Demote *me*? Mr. Numero-Uno salesperson? How crazy was this company?

But then I thought for a long moment. The company's reasons were sound. My interest in starting a professional speaking business had taken hold of me in the form of an exciting, vivid dream. I wanted to make it happen. Consequently my job selling advertising suffered. My body was going to work everyday, but my mind, my heart, and my soul were someplace else. I had let the fear of change stop me from making a change.

Talk about a wake-up call.

Finally I listened to my mind, heart, and soul. I was ready to tackle the dream of being a public speaker. I quit my great job and started my professional speaking business.

I haven't looked back since.

Reflection Exercise

Think back to a time when you were about to face a change or in the middle of facing a change? What were your fears at the time?

_____

_____

_____

Did these fears later come true?

_____

_____

_____

What helped you move successfully through the change?

_____

_____

_____

Could you apply one or more of these thoughts and ideas to another change situation?

_____

_____

_____

A Final Note

As you know, I'm an immigrant from a tiny village in Ghana, West Africa. Now when I used the word "immigrant" just now, what images entered your mind? Poor? Pitiful? Persecuted? Maybe all of these....

It's true that many immigrants to America are one or more of these things. But did you know that eighty percent of all millionaires in the United States right now are immigrants? That's right: four out of five.

Why is this? I have a theory. It consists of two parts. One, immigrants are willing to do all the jobs that people born in America won't do. They're not afraid of hard work or working a "demeaning" job. Success is a journey, and the immigrant knows that a person must start somewhere.

Secondly, immigrants are willing to change. In fact, they're more than willing; they embrace change, revel in it. Most have come from places far inferior to the United States in terms of quality of life, in the number of opportunities available. Change to these people is necessary, and they have learned from their change and now move forward with change all the time.

Discovering opportunities and living a life of change is all about attitude. In fact, I have a specific name for this: an Attitude of Gratitude.

Immigrants are grateful for the opportunities presented in America. They don't feel entitled to anything; they are not afraid to work toward their dreams and goals.

They embrace change as part of this Attitude of Gratitude.

The next time you are grumbling or complaining about something, stop and think, *Right now, do I have an Attitude of Gratitude?*

Develop an Attitude of Gratitude, and you will much more easily handle the pressures and challenges of change.

NOTES

CHAPTER 6

Becoming and Staying Motivated

I admire Harvey McKay. He's a successful businessman, author, and professional speaker. He's very motivating. I'm a motivated guy anyway, but I get even MORE motivated when I read or hear Harvey.

Here's one of Harvey's sayings:

Goal setting + Concentration + Determination = Success

I believe this is true. In Chapter Two, we talked about dreams and goals. And of course concentration is important to success. But what about determination? Everyone's determined, aren't they?

Yes and no.

Let me explain. I believe most people, when they first formulate a dream or goal, are very determined to move forward, to take action in a positive way. But then "things" happen…. It isn't always as easy as we first thought. Those darn obstacles pop up. One or more things go wrong. For every step taken forward, we seem to take two steps back. Our determination wanes.

A crucial element in personal and professional success is determination. I also call this staying motivated. Why is this so important? Because big goals and dreams will take weeks, months, even years to complete. Merely being "interested" in obtaining a dream isn't enough—a person has to stay motivated for the long-term, through the good and the bad, no matter what obstacles stand in the way.

Consider these successful people:

• At the age of 20, Tiger Woods burst into the professional golf world and begun winning tournaments almost immediately. A quick success? Hardly. Tiger had been playing golf since the age of two. He had already played in hundreds of tournaments around the world and spent countless hours on the practice range.

• Michael Jordan is considered by most to be the best basketball player of all time. His team won six championships in an eight-year stretch, and the two years they didn't, Michael had "retired" or was working his way back from "retirement." A quick success? Hardly. Michael played for years in the NBA before the Chicago Bulls won their first championship.

How to Stay Motivated

Here are twelve ways to stay motivated to move toward your dreams and goals.

1. Never Take Rejection Personally

Don't tell me I can't do something. Why? Because that makes me even *more* determined (motivated) to succeed. If someone tells you that you can't do something, ask them, "Why not?" Rejection is a fact of life. There are untold number of famous and successful authors, playwrights, script writers, dancers, performers, athletes and so on who were told "no" hundreds, even thousands, of times, but who kept on and eventually succeeded.

Most rejections aren't personal, i.e., the person saying "no" isn't criticizing you or your life, they are simply passing on your work or idea. As much as possible, separate what it is that you do or want to have happen with your core being, the person you are.

Instead of taking rejection personally, attempt to learn from it. Ask yourself these questions:

Is this rejection valid?

If so, what must I do to improve or otherwise strengthen what I have to offer?

If I don't feel the rejection is valid, what other person/organization should I instead ask?

2. Surround Yourself with Positive People

Staying motivated is difficult, especially for the "long haul" or when things get tough. But having a support group, people who are positive and enthusiastic, will help you regain and strengthen your motivation and enthusiasm. Find people who are positive in their attitudes and supportive of your efforts. Ask these people for help, even if it's "just to chat."

Above all, avoid people who are negative, pessimistic, or generally unhappy. (I call these people "Dream Busters" — avoid them like the plague!)

Reflective Exercise

Who are positive people in your life that you can go to now for support and inspiration?

_____

....

_____

Who are people whose attitudes aren't positive, who you would be best to avoid if possible?

_____

....

....

---

3. Always Believe in Yourself

There will be times when self-doubt creeps in. It happens to everyone. Remember the 4 a.m. wake-up call we discussed in Chapter 3?

Banish self-doubt. Always believe in yourself and your abilities. You may not have achieved "success"—yet—but you do have many positive, constructive qualities that are helping you and others.

It's funny, but I'm a firm believer that a person can have just about anything on earth if they first mentally accept the fact that they can have it. If you want success, think of yourself as a success. The feeling of success and the positive messages you are sending your brain and body will help you create success.

The only thing that stands between you and what you want from life is simply the will to pursue your dreams and the faith to believe that your dreams can come true.

4. Build on Past Successes

For most of us, self-doubt is a powerful force. It's always there, lurking, somewhere. Believing in yourself is one way to banish self-doubt. Another way is to focus on your past successes and accomplishments and use these positive feelings to help you stay motivated.

But Albert, I don't have any past successes to build on.

That's not true. Did you graduate from high school? How about college? Have you had a job before, one that you did at least well enough to remain employed? Ever had a good friend, someone you trusted and who trusted you? Have you ever played on a sports team, worked in a positive environment, helped another succeed or overcome a problem? Sure you have.

Past successes are important for two reasons. One, they help you realize that you can succeed, that success is part of who you are. *If I did that before, I can certainly do this.*

Secondly, think of past successes as steps. Your dream may look far away, way up there in the sky. But remember this: Almost no one gains their success with one giant leap. It takes steps. Many steps. Take one small step at time. Build on each success.

5. Always Give of Yourself Freely

To reach your dreams and goals, you will need help from others. Likewise, throughout your life you will have the opportunity to help others. This is what I mean to "give of yourself freely"—help as many others as possible. Don't worry that the time spent helping them will take away from your goals and desires. What you give away will be returned to you a thousand times over.

Reflective Exercise

Who are some of the people that you've helped, in one form or another?

_____

_____

_____

Now list those you can help:

_____

_____

_____

Please note that some people have a difficult time asking for help. They don't want to bother another person, or feel that asking for help is a sign of weakness. Offer your assistance to others even if they have not asked for help. Show that you care, and that you can be a resource in their own personal journey. Many times, just knowing a friend has offered to help, should the need arise, is all the support a person needs to succeed.

6. Plan Your Work and Work Your Plan

No matter how vivid or defined your dreams and goals are, a person must still take daily action toward achieving them. What's more, this daily action must be *focused* on specific tasks needed to help achieve a dream or goal.

A haphazard approach simply won't work. Have a plan to do the tasks that you need to do to succeed, then work hard at executing this plan. Use whatever system or program you need to make your plan easy to understand and simple to follow. Many use "to-do" lists, appointment calendars, or other written methods. The computer, when used correctly, can be a resource to schedule tasks, activities, and appointments. Whatever way you use to record your plan, make certain that is simple, easily accessible at all times, and that you understand it.

Having a plan also aids greatly when a setback occurs. Have you missed a couple of work days because of an illness? Heard "no" from an important person or opportunity? Seen something that you tried for the first time not go as well as expected?

Get back on plan. Review your dreams and goals, and your plan, and then figure out exactly what are the next steps that you should be taking to again be working your work.

Plan your work, and work your plan, and you will stay on the path to success.

7. Always Confront Your Doubts

In these times of massive changes, you will face difficulties, obstacles, and your own internal doubts. Don't hide from these things, most of all your doubts. Face your difficulties. Draw on the courage inside you that resides in the reserves of your mind, which are more powerful and uplifting than any outside circumstances.

When you are bigger than your problems, you'll find the courage necessary to win. If you confront your fears, and do so often, you'll program yourself to succeed.

8. Move Forward Daily

I've said it before, but it needs repeating: Take daily action toward your goals. Success isn't achieved in a "flash of inspiration," like a bolt of lighting thrown from the sky. No, success is made up of small, daily steps that little by little, inch by inch, move us to success.

Many people I speak to come up to me afterward and say, "But Albert, I don't have the *patience* to do all the little things" or "But Albert, I don't have the *time* to do all the little things."

You must learn to develop the patience for success, and you must make the time on a daily basis to work toward your goals.

You may be a mother, and have a full or part-time job, but you can still carve out fifteen minutes a day to read about what it is that you want to become.

You may be a father, with a busy career, but you can still carve out thirty minutes a day to study for the test to enter law school.

You may be a student, with a full-time job to support your studies, but you can still carve out twenty minutes a day to paint watercolors.

Will these snippets lead to anything valuable? Yes, over time they will. If you spent thirty minutes a day focused and working toward a goal or dream, think what you could accomplish in:

> ... a week
>
> ... a month
>
> ... a year
>
> ...five years

Remember, a journey of a thousand miles begins with one step.

9. Have a Role Model

A role model is someone who you can look to for inspiration and information on how to succeed. Ideally your role model is someone you know and can meet with, such as a family member or colleague at work. Attempt to meet with this person on a regular basis, such as once a week or once every couple of months (how often you meet will depend upon where the person lives in relationship to you and the relationship that the two of you have). Ask your role model questions about their successes, what they focus on, how they move toward dreams and goals. If appropriate, ask advice about a particular problem or challenge you are facing.

A role model can be a person that you do not know, such as a famous athlete or world leader. You can still benefit by learning all you can about the person and their beliefs, attitudes, and actions. How? Read about them; watch them on television or listen to them on the radio; read the books or articles or papers they have written. The key here is to not pick someone that is so obscure that no real information exists by or about them. Still not convinced? Think what you could learn by studying what has been written about or by:

- Bill Gates, co-founder of Microsoft
- Jack Welch, current Chairman of General Electric
- Oprah Winfrey, talk show wonder host
- Mia Hamm, considered by many as the best women's soccer player in the world

Don't limit yourself to successful business people or athletes. What about:

- Mother Teresa
- The Dali Lama
- Picasso
- Rosa Parks
- Nelson Mandela
- John F. Kennedy
- Jacqueline Kennedy
- Your father
- Your mother
- One of your grandparents
- Dr. Kwame Nkrumah

Find a role model and learn from them.

10. Don't Sweat the Bad Days

Dr. Richard Carlson has written a series of books that all begin "Don't Sweat…." I'll tag-on and say this: Don't worry about a bad day. Every day isn't going to be your best. You might not be feeling physically well. You might be tired. You might simply be a little "down."

The important thing is to know that these days will happen—they happen to everyone—and instead of worrying or fretting, move on as best as possible. Focus on the end of your journey. Don't worry about this one particular day. There will be many, many other days that will more than make-up for this one bad day.

11. Cherish Your Unique Qualities

One of the most amazing things about success, both personal and professional, is that no two people reach success in exactly the same way. Of the billions of people on this earth, you are unique. No one else is exactly like you. No one is even close.

Use this uniqueness to your advantage. Gather inspiration, information, even suggestions from friends and role models, but solve problems in your own way. Don't worry about your differences; expand on them.

12. The Mind is What Drives a Person

Ever heard this computer term "GIGO-Garbage In, Garbage Out"?

Of course you have. Your mind is like a computer; it processes and uses the information and thoughts you feed it. Fill your mind with negative thoughts, and you will act negatively. Fill it with positive thoughts, and you will act positively.

Simple? Yes it is, but let me tell you this: IT'S ALSO TRUE!

Here are a few ways I attempt to feed my mind daily (even hourly) doses of what I call "let's go info!":

- Begin with waking up. Don't grumble at the alarm and roll over; smile at the alarm, think immediately of something positive that you have planned for the day ahead, mediate on this positive thing for a few minutes. Then get out of bed ready to go at it.

- Keep a file or notebook of uplifting quotes. Read through these frequently. Always be adding new quotes and clips from other sources, such as magazines, newspaper articles, notes you taken when speaking with someone...or from this book!

- Read biographies of great people. I can almost guarantee you that you will learn two things when reading biographies: you will learn something about how to achieve success, and you will learn that every successful person had to overcome not one, or two, but many significant and troublesome problems to succeed.

Review and follow these twelve suggestions, and you'll stay motivated, excited, even passionate about your dreams and goals.

A Final Note

As you can see, I know that having an exciting, vivid dream or goal isn't enough: a person must become and stay motivated to work toward that dream or goal. It's tough to stay motivated. Success often takes years of hard work, toil. The information in this chapter will help, but here's something else I'd like to share. I call it having a "laugh attack."

When I'm feeling down or discouraged, often a peppy motivational quote isn't enough. Talk is cheap, right? And reading about someone else's success can create thoughts such as, "Am I the only non-winner out there?"

But I've found one thing that almost always recharges my motivation: laughter. If I get myself laughing, in a few minutes I've got my enthusiasm back and I'm ready to press on.

Here are suggestions on how to add laughter to your life:

- Keep a book of jokes or one written by your favorite comedic actor or actress nearby, and refer to it frequently. Bill Cosby and Jerry Seinfeld are two who have written *very* funny books.

- Keep videos handy of favorite funny movies or television shows. Pop in "Caddyshack" or an old "I Love Lucy" rerun and see if you can watch the entire show *without* laughing. That's right: Try <u>not</u> to laugh. Impossible, right?

- Play with your kids. Role around the floor. Have a tickling contest. Play hide and seek. Pretend you're eight years old again, or six, or four. (If you don't have any kids, play with nieces or nephews or others with whom you have a trusting relationship.)

- Get out and find laughs. Go to a funny movie. Go see a comedy play being performed. Attend a comedy club. Get out with others laughing and having a good time; it's hard *not* to feel good with the right atmosphere.

Laughter helps by giving you a break from the daily world and its pressures and challenges. When you're finished with your "break," I'm certain that you'll find yourself much more positive and much more motivated to again work on—no, *attack with passion*—your goals, dreams, and plans needed for success.

NOTES

CHAPTER 7

Connecting with Others

African Proverb:
A man with no friends has no one to help him up.

Let me tell you about the day Molly got shot.

As you've probably seen or guessed by now, I'm a black man. I've experienced prejudice. I've definitely been prejudice. Nobody escapes it, in my opinion. Nobody.

Let me tell you about a time that my own prejudice almost got the better of me.

It's Christmas Eve, and I'm out doing some last minute Christmas shopping. (This won't surprise the people who know me!) Anyway, by early evening I'm tired of fighting the crowds and the traffic and the rain and rushing around, so I decide to get a haircut, relax for a few minutes. I drive to a part of Seattle that's called South Ranier Beach, because I know there's a good barbershop there. Now those of you who don't know much about Seattle, South Ranier Beach is considered a low-income section of the city. It's a rough place. Good people, good businesses, but rough.

Anyway, I drive to the barbershop and luckily find a parking spot right outside for Molly. You see, Molly is my loving, faithful Jeep Cherokee. Molly and I go way back. I can't imagine my life without Molly in it.

So I'm sitting inside having my hair cut when we all hear a loud noise. BAMMMMM!

Everyone jumps up to see what happened. Everyone that is, except me; I'm ducking behind the counter. I mean, this is South Ranier Beach, right? I think it's a gunshot. I *know* it's a gunshot. *What am I doing down here after dark?* I'm asking myself.

Finally somebody yells out that my car has been hit. I jump up and look out. Sure enough, there's Molly, hurt, angry. Her front bumper is gone; there's water and green antifreeze seeping out of her. My MOLLY! She's in PAIN!

A man driving a big old-fashioned van has bumped into Molly. Now picture this scene. The driver of the van is white. Six or seven people who were inside the barbershop, all of whom happen to be black, rush outside. Others in the neighborhood, most of whom are black, start to gather. And they start shouting.

"Get him before he gets away!"

"Fry his butt!"

"Let's make him pay!"

I look inside at the van driver. He's so scared he's shaking. *Shaking.* Hard.

This was my moment of choice.

This poor guy had just done serious damage to my beloved Molly. I could jump all over his case. Make him sweat, make him scared, maybe make him beg for forgiveness.

But I didn't do any of those things. I asked myself this question: How would I want to be treated in a situation like this?

And that made all the difference.

I calmed my friends down, then offered the driver a smile and invited him to step outside of the van and work things out.

But the driver wasn't ready to believe me. Not just yet. In fact, it probably would've been easier to ask him to donate an arm or a leg to a limb bank than to step out of that van. So I keep smiling, saying we'll work it out, and finally he does step out.

The first thing I say to him is this: "Hey, don't worry. That's why we pay big bucks to the insurance companies, right? You do have insurance, right?"

He has insurance. We work things out.

Do you see what happened here? I could have blown my fuse, especially as a black man who has been discriminated against, as a black man now confronting a white man. But I didn't blow up. I made another choice: I tried to connect.

Here's my definition of what it means to connect with another person:

When we *connect* with another person, we treat them with the same courtesy, respect and understanding that we would want to be treated.

Connecting with others isn't easy. I'm not saying it is. It's fraught with miscommunication, misconceptions, missed opportunities. Don't try for perfection. None of us is perfect. Try for connection. Remember:

Connection, not perfection.

Reflective Exercise

Think of someone with whom you share a good connection. How does this special connection make you feel?

_____

_____

_____

_____

Now think of someone who you don't have a good connection with, but wished that you did.

What happened?

_____

_____

_____

What action can you take TODAY to strengthen the connection?

_____

_____

_____

_____

How to Connect

Here are my suggestions on ways to connect with others, particularly business colleagues and even clients:

- Listen to the other person. Don't just listen, with your mind wandering or worrying about what you are going to say next. LISTEN. Make eye contact. Focus on what the person is saying. Don't prejudge. Resist the urge to begin formulating what it is that you're going to say.

- Be a resource. Connecting with people means that you like them and will, if possible, assist them. When someone asks for your help or assistance, avoid the "I'm too busy right now" pat answer. If at all possible, make the time. If not, suggest another way that you could help or someone else who might possibly be able to assist the person. Not only will you be helping another person, one day you might need that very person's assistance in some small—or large—way.

- Be authentic. Connecting with others isn't about being phony, about telling jokes at the water cooler or swapping information about the local sports team. No, it's about being yourself, sharing a part of yourself. So many of us hide our true selves behind a mask. Open up. Risk connecting with others. Share a part of yourself that others might not normally see.

A Final Note

Here's another phrase that I like and attempt to live by:

SERVICE BEFORE SELF

That's what connecting with others is all about, isn't it? Yes, you benefit in terms of friendship and support. But it's really all about helping others, right?

YES!

The next time someone asks you for help, be it a friend or business colleague, even your kids with their homework, before you reply say these three words to yourself:

SERVICE BEFORE SELF

I guarantee you that your answer will be different than what you normally would have said.

A Final Note

The stories I have told here, in this book, I have lived. They are events from my life. You may be saying, *Yes, Albert, I like the stories, but I wasn't there so I can't fully relate.*

Wrong. In a larger sense, you've been there.

- Have you ever been inspired by a movie you saw, a book you read? If so, then you were with me in that movie theater when I was eight years old and my dream of one day going to America first materialized.

- Have you ever felt a moment of liberation over fear, when you said to yourself, "This time, I will not run!"? Then you were with me at the river's edge, staring down that snake.

- Have you ever been treated as a problem, as an outsider, rather than as a person? Then you were in that bank with me when I tried to open up an account with that first unhelpful teller.

- Have you ever been faced with choice between personal gain and helping another? Then you were with me when my pregnant wife's water broke, and I decided to go to my "important" meeting instead.

I hope this book has been a source of inspiration and help for you. The material here means a great deal to me. In addition to sharing stories from my life, I am attempting to live the ideas and suggestions I have presented. It is a challenge. For the past two years of my life as I've started my professional speaking career, I've experienced many peaks and valleys. I've had horrible self-doubts, the kind that can crush a dream.

But, I am proud to say, I have persevered, and so must you.

Thank you for taking the time to let me share with you my stories, thoughts, and ideas. Writing this book has been a wonderful opportunity for me. I truly hope it helps you become an Opportunist and open up many exciting, wonderful opportunities as well.

Each of us must be committed to keep dreaming, to keep persevering.

Each of us in this constantly-changing world must always be looking for opportunities…to advance, make money, grow, to create success…and even more important, to bring love and light to the world.

Thank you.

P.S. I would love to learn about your own stories and challenges when creating and facing opportunities, fears, and dreams. Please e-mail me at the following:

Albert@questforyourbest.com

About the Author

*"Opportunities in this changing world are everywhere.
But they are invisible to the person who is not
clear what it is that they want."*
— Albert Mensah

Albert Mensah began his journey to success in one of the most impoverished nations in the world: Ghana, in West Africa. His is a story of triumph over adversity, of the power of a dream to mold a person's character, of a will strong enough to shape a destiny.

Growing up, Albert's family, like many in his tiny village, had no electricity and no running water. One of his boyhood chores was to walk eight miles every morning to fetch the firewood and water his family needed for cooking and bathing. At the age of eight, his family moved to Ghana's largest city, Accra. Shortly after moving, Albert saw his first film, an American movie, and a dream was born: to venture to America and live among its people and the many opportunities available to all.

For ten years, Albert pursued his dream. He studied English, wrote to American pen pals, befriended American priests at the local Jesuit high school. In 1978, Albert's dream came true: he won a full four-year scholarship to Western Maryland College.

Albert Mensah is someone who not only sees opportunity, he acts on opportunity. After graduating from college, he moved up in a series of jobs, eventually culminating as a top sales producer for US West, where he achieved numerous "number one" rankings and constantly exceeded his sales quotas. On a personal level, he married his college sweetheart. They live outside Seattle with their two children.

Two years ago, a new dream found Albert: To share his stories of inspiration and success with others. To do so, Albert began his own business and became a professional speaker.

The results have been nothing short of phenomenal. He has spoken to scores of organizations and thousands of people, sharing a message of inspiration and opportunity. In 1999, he was runner-up in the Toastmasters *International World Championship of Professional Speaking* contest.

Albert Mensah began his journey in the humblest of settings. Now he has reached the highest levels of personal and professional success. His passion is to share his stories and insights that will help others see and act on opportunities, reach their dreams, and become the people they want to become.

About This Book

This book costs $14.95.
To order a copy, send a check for
$17.95 ($14.95 plus $3.00 p/h)
made payable to Albert Mensah to:

Albert Mensah/Quest for Your Best
P.O. Box 94308
Seattle, WA 98124-6608
www.questforyourbest.com

Please allow 2-4 weeks for delivery.

For special pricing for quantities
greater than 10, please call

888-255-3925

or e-mail

albert@questforyourbest.com

Albert is also available for
speaking engagements,
workshops, and individual consulting.

Contact him today to discuss your needs.

Thank you!

Albert Mensah

Professional Speaker/Author

Engaging personality • Professional delivery • Quality content

What Others Are Saying About...ALBERT MENSAH

"Very charismatic."
—**Les Brown**, motivational speaker and author of
It's Not Over Until You Win

• • • • •

"...a great and inspiring speaker."
—**Mark Victor Hansen**, co-author of
Chicken Soup for the Soul

• • • • •

"Mesmerizing, expressive,...passionate.
You have something special."
—**Rosita Perez**, professional speaker

• • • • •

"...the audience who witnessed your presentation was
motivated and awed by the experiences and ideas
you shared. Thank you for sharing your talents."
—**Roy Morton**, The Boeing Company
(loaned executive at The United Way)

• • • • •

"You truly have a gift. I give you an A+!"
—**Pamela Baade**,
The Weyerhaeuser Corporation

• • • • •

"The level of giving from our employees after your dynamic speech
increased twenty-three percent. We're positive that your
speech was the catalyst for our campaign success."
—**Lisa Byerly**, Campaign Coordinator,
Regence Blue Shield